CU00941559

DISCLAIMER AND/OR LEGAL NOTICES.

While all attempts have been made to verify information provided in this book and its
ancillary materials, neither the author or publisher assumes any responsibility for
errors, inaccuracies or omissions and is not responsible for any financial loss by
customer in any manner. Any slights of people or organizations are unintentional. If
advice concerning legal, financial, accounting or related matters is needed, the services
of a qualified professional should be sought. This book and its associated ancillary
materials, including verbal and written training, is not intended for use as a source of
legal, financial or accounting advice. You should be aware of the various laws
governing business transactions or other business practices in your particular
geographical location.

EARNINGS & INCOME DISCLAIMER

With respect to the reliability, accuracy, timeliness, usefulness, adequacy,
completeness, and/ or suitability of information provided in this book, Diana
Herrington, RFFL, its partners, associates, affiliates, consultants, and/or presenters
make no warranties, guarantees, representations, or claims of any kind. Readers'
results will vary depending on a number of factors. Any and all claims or
representations as to income earnings are not to be considered as average earnings.
Testimonials are not representative. This book and all products and services are for
educational and informational purposes only. Use caution and see the advice of
qualified professionals. Check with your accountant, attorney or professional advisor
before acting on this or any information. You agree that Diana Herrington and/or
RFFL is not responsible for the success or failure of your personal, business, health or
financial decisions relating to any information presented by Diana Herrington, RFFL,
or company products/services. Earnings potential is entirely dependent on the efforts,
skills and application of the individual person. Any examples, stories, references, or
case studies are for illustrative purposes only and should not be interpreted as
testimonies and/or examples of what reader and/or consumers can generally expect
from the information. No representation in any part of this information, materials
and/or seminar training are guarantees or promises for actual performance. Any
statements, strategies, concepts, techniques, exercises and ideas in the information,
materials and/or seminar training offered are simply opinion or experience, and thus
should not be misinterpreted as promises, typical results or guarantees (expressed or
implied). The author and publisher (Diana Herrington, RFFL or any of RFFL's
representatives) shall in no way, under any circumstances, be held liable to any party
(or third party) for any direct, indirect, punitive, special, incidental or other
consequential damages arising directly or indirectly from any use of books, materials
and or seminar trainings, which is provided "as is," and without warranties.

MEDICAL WARNING and DISCLAIMER:

The information in this book is not intended as medical advice or to replace a one-on-
one relationship with a qualified health care professional. It is intended as a sharing of
knowledge and information from the research and experience of Diana Herrington. We
encourage you to make your own health care decisions.

WHAT OTHERS ARE SAYING ABOUT
(Real Food for Life) &
(Diana Herrington) STRATEGIES

"If you want a powerful long-term health strategy and are tired of trying trends that haven't worked, read and apply the time-tested principles in Diana Herrington's book. Diana is not just offering you nice theories. She lives these principles wholeheartedly and is one the healthiest living eaters I know. I have watched Diana transform from a weak feeble lady who could barely sit up in a chair in my living room to a powerful lady who speeds around Edmonton with flair."

~ Randy Fritz
Health Consultant

"I lost weight 2 lbs. I feel healthier, lighter, not bloated and no hunger pains. Having a schedule and recipes to follow on your course Diana that I knew were balanced and made me feel good.

~ June Benaschak,
RFFL Fall Cleanse

"Diana has provided me with support that only someone with her wealth of knowledge could give. Her straightforward and simple concepts have greatly benefited me. I'm thankful for her being there, especially while dealing with my body health."

~ Heidi Van Heukelom,
Consultation

"Diana's suggestions for improving my food combinations helped to lighten my digestion and support my ability to fall asleep more easily at night. Her easy to follow recipes help me to make healthy choices that taste great and make me feel good!"

~ Maureen Doram, Health
Food Advocate for 30+ years

"It is, indeed a pleasure to know Diana. Her knowledge in the field of health and wellness is exceptional. I have adjusted my diet using her input and recipes to maintain my good health."
~ Wayne Rogers P Eng.
LC Luminessence Inc

"In the short time I have been working with Diana, her generosity and wealth of knowledge and experience have been instrumental to me in making healthy choices every day; I feel lucky to have such a positive mentor and friend in her."
~ Kevin Parkinson,
Consultation

"I've noticed (and my husband has noticed changes in my appearance) since doing this Real Food for Life program. I don't feel hungry and am really enjoying the simplicity of the 'plates'. I've noticed the 'love handles around my waist seem to be shrinking. I'm definitely getting results. Thanks!'
~ Ann Humble
Health Advocate &
Consultant

"Understanding the food combinations has impacted my life. I'm more aware of what I eat, when and how I feel. Eating protein and carbs together is a ticket for heartburn and indigestion for me. I now understand why and I can avoid this without using antacids or digestive enzymes. !"
~ Doreen Kelsey
RFFL Healthy Diet Course

"I have been following Diana's website Real Food for Life since 2017, after reading her informative post about olive oil. Diana has remarkable insight about nutrition that you will not find on mainstream health websites. She takes a holistic approach to health that can easily be incorporated into one's lifestyle."
~ Adrian Lewis
Health and Fitness Writer

"I have lost another five pounds (lost 10 pound the first Real Food for Life course). I learned that I can eat fruit without feeling guilty. You just have to know when to eat it and now I know!"

~Domine King

RFFL Spring Cleanse

"Well you will do Amazing with this book love your recipes and all the knowledge that you share. Your food is always Healthy & Delicious thank you for everything that you do to make sure we can eat such great foods."
`

~ Marilyn Hogan

Medical Intuitive

"I care about my health. Diana is able to help me find the right foods with exciting recipes. I'm an artist of poetry and music but have learned to use a creative bent when cooking. Diana provides many imaginative dishes. Really great site you have created here Thanks for working so hard to share this important information."

~ Dani Zyp

Artist and Writer

"My favorite recipe on your course is the Autumn Crunchy Salad. I love that warm tahini dressing! I lost five pounds and have more energy! I am Inspired to make some small daily changes like eating more fruit".

~ Debra Martin,

RFFL Fall Cleanse

"For over 23 years, I've witnessed Diana's remarkable journey in natural health. She's more than an expert; she's a life-changer. Her website and articles have been a go-to for healthy living. I've seen her turn a grave health condition around, inspiring many, including myself. Together, Diana and I have presented our knowledge to eager audiences in various forms and places and she always leaves them wanting more of her natural healing wisdom. Diana is a true pioneer in the natural health world."

~ Rob Cooper

Web Coach

THE IDEAL PROFESSIONAL SPEAKER FOR YOUR NEXT EVENT!

Any organization that wants to help people become "very healthy eaters" needs to Hire **Diana Herrington** for a keynote and/or workshop training!
She has taught many online courses and spoken at events.

TO CONTACT OR BOOK
Diana Herrington
TO SPEAK:

diana@realfoodforlife.com

THE IDEAL
HEALTH
COACH
FOR YOU!

If you're ready to overcome your eating challenges, have major breakthroughs and achieve higher levels, then you will love having Diana Herrington as your coach!

TO CONTACT
Diana Herrington
diana@realfoodforlife.com

Dedication

It is with respect, admiration and sincere appreciation, that I dedicate this book to my wonderful friends and family. Without you and the lessons you have taught me throughout my life, I would not have the blessing of being where I am today. Thank you from the bottom of my heart! I love you dearly!
These five wonderful people have all been very helpful in the journey of writing this book.

Randy Fritz truly got me writing and getting this book onto the Real Food for Life website. It's been selling as a pdf since 2011. He has been supportive of what I am doing in many ways. He is a good friend too.

 April Dery, thank you to my sweet sister for editing this book a few years ago. She also gave me many health tip to research. It's sad that she won't be seeing this as she passed away last year.

Rob Cooper has been a great help as what I call a website guru. He has done much to make it all work well and given me extra helpful tips. Also, because he has much health knowledge he is inspiring.

 Adrian Lewis is a social media genius and has helped me in so many ways to keep it all flowing for Real Food for Life. He's been right here for me getting this book ready to be a Bestseller on Amazon.

Ann Humble helped edit and proof read the first book 'Eating Green Clean and Lean'. It's been selling on the website as a pdf since 2011. Also, she helped make a health event happen for Real Food for Life!

Table of Contents

A Message to You!

This is my story of how I went from dealing with a difficult health challenge to living vibrantly healthy. May you find my story heartwarming and inspiring!

In 1996, I was living in England suffering from severe chronic fatigue syndrome and fibromyalgia weighing 94 pounds. At five foot six inches, this meant that I was underweight and malnourished.

I'd lose a couple of pounds a week. My doctor didn't know how to help me. He said I'd eventually be put into a hospital to be on intravenous for nourishment.

My naturopathic doctor suggested I go to Scott's Natural Health Institutein Ohio to do a water fast. He knew my body needed a deep cleanse and best to be overseen.

Deciding to go on this journey of only drinking water was scary, due to being so underweight and unable to walk well. Yet, there didn't seem to be any other helpful options.

Some people thought I had anorexia. I'd eat but my body didn't accept food as my digestion was poor.There were only 12 foods that I could eat and often couldn't even tolerate them. I would have extreme indigestion, with a deep stomach ache after eating one of them.

I tried many remedies that didn't help which cost a small fortune. What I learned was to accept what is happening and be open and available for my body to heal while doing my best. I decided to do the water fast at the institute.

At the end of the water fast it was time to be on a nourishing program for 10 days. During this time Dr Scott taught me how to get the most nutrition out of the food I was eating. His teaching included the principles of Food combining and Acid/Alkaline Balance.

I left the clinic weighing 98 pounds and was able to eat 12 foods successfully daily.Both principles helped me regain my health more than anything else I had tried. I'm so grateful to Dr Scott. Learning about the principle of Acid/Alkaline Balance was the beginning of a health makeover.

I went from 20 – 30% functioning to 40 – 50% which was the beginning of a journey to being fully healthy in 2001 and now able to go for 1 to 2 hours walks regularly.

The above is from a book I'm writing: **'Was Sick and Tired – Now Dancing in Life'**. Here's where you can learn more. www.realfoodforlife.com/my-fibromyalgia-story

"Diana Herrington turned a debilitating health crisis into a passion for helping others with healthy, sugar-free, gluten-free, eating and cooking. After testing and researching every possible healthy therapy on her delicate system she has developed simple, powerful principles which she shares in her books and website." – Randy Fritz

In 2002 I registered Real Food for Life with GoDaddy. Sharing what I learned about food and health was important. In 2004 I became a host for 2 large groups Healthy Living Network and Healthy Cooking of 5,000 members on **Care2** and a **Greenliving Writer** for Care2's over 51 million members. Also, wrote for four local publications.

In 2009 I created the Real Food for Life website with Randy Fritz. So grateful, for his help in making it happen.
It's all about eating Real Food.

SECRET ONE

Balance Your Body
All You Need to Know About the Alkaline Diet

This principle was a life changer for me. It helped me get my health back and be fully active in this wonderful life.

I've seen it make a big healthy difference in many people's lives that have worked with me in courses and coaching.

What is Alkaline and Acid in Your Body Mean?

Alkaline/acid diets are based on serious chemistry which is puzzling for most of us.

There is information out there saying to go fully alkaline. That is not a healthy way. It is all about eating a balanced diet of alkaline and acid.

> "Every organ system in your body depends on pH balance. But your lungs and kidneys work to regulate it." ~ WebMD Editorial Contributors

Alkaline and acids can seem to be opposing but our body needs both to be fully functioning. When there is a balance with acid and alkaline the body is actually in an Acid-Alkaline Balance meaning healthy.

The good news is: you do not need to be a scientist or chemist to understand the benefits of a balanced alkaline/acid diet. All you need is an Acid/Alkaline chart and to be willing to try new ways of eating.

Did you know that the water fish swim in, needs to have the correct pH balance to live?

Also, plants flourish when the soil is at the right pH level. Life thrives when there's balance.

Let's begin by learning why this way of eating is very important in helping you experience vibrant health.

10 Benefits of Having
A Balanced Acid/Alkaline Body

1. More elastic, youthful looking skin.
2. Deeper and more restful sleep.
3. Abundant physical energy.
4. Fewer colds, headaches, and flues.
5. Excellent digestion.
6. Less arthritis.
7. Reduction of candida (yeast) overgrowth.
8. Helps prevent osteoporosis.
9. Increased mental acuity and mental alertness.
10. Legal natural high.

Your body is totally regulated by pH! Is your diet balanced?

It's all about eating lots of vegetables and fruits, drinking lots of pure water.

Acid is for Your Car Battery Not Your Body!

Check Out This List of Symptoms of Being Too Acidic

1. **Digestive issues:**
   - Excess stomach acid.
   - Acid reflux.
   - Gastritis.
   - Ulcers.
   - Saliva acidic.

2. **Unhealthy Skin, Nails and Hair:**
   - Nails are thin and break easily.
   - Dry skin.
   - Cracks at the corners of the lips.
   - Hair is dull with split ends, and falls out.
   - Hives.
   - Very pale face.

3. **Teeth and Mouth Issues:**
   - Loose teeth.
   - Teeth sensitive to hot, cold, or acidic foods.
   - Teeth have a tendency to crack or chip.
   - Sensitive gums.
   - Mouth ulcers.
   - Infections in throat and tonsils.
   - Tooth nerve pain.

4. **Eyes, Head and General Body:**
   - Headaches.
   - Low body temperature (feels cold).
   - Tendency to get infections.
   - Leg cramps and spasms.
   - Eyes tear easily, conjunctivitis, inflammation of the eyelids and corneas.

5. **Nerves and Emotions:**
   - Low energy; constant fatigue.
   - Being continually depressed with a loss of joy and enthusiasm.
   - Excessive nervousness

What Research and Experts Say and Do

Here is a good summary of what research says by Dr Ax. https://draxe.com/nutrition/alkaline-diet/ "A 2012 review published in the *Journal of Environmental Health* found that achieving pH balance by eating an alkaline diet can be helpful in reducing morbidity and mortality from numerous chronic diseases and ailments — such as hypertension, diabetes, arthritis, vitamin D deficiency and low bone density, just to name a few."

1. **An overly acidic condition weakens the body and can become dangerous.** Our body requires a slightly alkaline condition to function well. Blood, for example, needs to be 7.4 pH. A shift in blood pH of just 0.2 could result in death. Obviously, the body does not want to die so it is forced to borrow minerals which are alkaline (calcium, sodium, potassium and magnesium) from vital organs and bones to neutralize the acid.

2. Many of the hip fractures among middle-aged women are connected to high acidity caused by **a diet rich in animal foods and low in vegetables**. A seven-year study conducted at the University of California, on 9,000 women showed that those who have chronic acidosis are at greater risk for bone loss than those who have normal pH levels. - *American Journal of Clinical Nutrition*

3. "The countless names of illnesses do not really matter. What does matter is that they all come from the same root cause...too much tissue acid waste in the body!" says **Dr. Theodore A. Baroody** in his book *Alkalize or Die.*

4. "**Immune cells that are too acid** or too alkaline do not produce antibodies or cytokines (chemical messengers to regulate other immune cells), and they have impaired phagocytosis (the ability to engulf and destroy microbes). As a result, the affected individual becomes susceptible to viral, bacterial, fungal and other infectious microbes as well as cancer." Says **Dr. William Lee Cowden.**

5. **Acidosis increases insulin resistance**, which can lead to type-2 diabetes and possibility of having kidney stones and kidney failure according to Dr. Anthony Sebastian, University of California, and San Francisco. He goes on to say that one study suggests that being to acidic may alter gene activity and raise the risk of breast cancer.

6. "Consider that **Americans consume more calcium-rich dairy foods than almost every other nation, and we have one of the highest rates of osteoporosis**, dairy may be rich in calcium, but most dairy foods also produce an acid yield."says Loren Cordain, Ph.D., professor/researcher in the department of health science at Colorado State University.

7. Janet was diagnosed at 52 with osteopenia, which often leads to osteoporosis. At 55, Janet began following Dr Susan Brown's recommendations for eating more fruits and vegetables, taking supplements, and exercising. **After three years, Janet was building bone mass in her spine and hip while going through menopause.** Dr Susan Brown is from the Osteoporosis Education Project in East Syracuse, N.Y.

8. 'Acidosis is caused by an overproduction of acid that builds up in the blood or an excessive loss of bicarbonate from the blood (metabolic acidosis) or by a buildup of carbon dioxide in the blood that results from poor lung function or depressed breathing (respiratory acidosis)."
Says James L. Lewis III, MD

9. **An alkaline forming diet will help in preventing and treating osteoporosis,** age related muscle wasting, calcium kidney stones, exercise-induced asthma and slow the progression of age related chronic renal insufficiency according to a paper in the American Journal of Clinical Nutrition called 'Origins and evolution of the Western diet: health implications for the 21st century'.

10. **To prevent or treat acidosis or alkalosis,** naturopathic doctors often recommend changing the diet to more fruits and vegetables which are alkaline forming.

11. **Cures for an acid stomach** include increasing consumption of raw fruits and vegetables (alkaline forming foods) in Ayurvedic (traditional Indian) medicine. Ayurvedic healers have an understanding of the basic underlying principles of acidity and alkalinity; they say an excess of acid in the body related to having certain body type known as a 'pitta dosha'.

12. **Cancer and Alkaline Balance**
    - "Studies of isolated cell cultures and animal studies of cancer don't necessarily represent what happens within the human body. If the area in the body around tumors is more acidic, that doesn't mean that an acidic body environment caused the cancer. Rather, it could be a result of cancer cells' high metabolic rate that generates acids (like lactic acid). In a large population study, scores representing a higher dietary acid load were linked with increased risk of type 2 diabetes. Since that review, an observational study found that diets categorized as more acid-producing were associated with increased risk, and alkaline diets were associated with decreased risk" Says Karen Collins, MS, RDN, CDN, FAND
    - A balanced body, not highly acidic one makes it easier for cells to cleanse out waste and toxins. Thus a balanced alkaline pH will help in protecting the cells in your body and may discourage the growth of cancer cells.

How do We Balance Our pH?

Our typical diet consists mostly of acid forming foods (proteins, cereals, sugars, fats and chemicals). It does not mean that all acid forming foods are unhealthy; it is the balance we are looking for. Alkaline foods such as vegetables and fruit are often eaten in much smaller quantities; not enough to neutralize the excess of the acid forming foods we consume. Also, common habits like coffee, tea, alcohol and tobacco, are extremely acidifying.

Our body is approximately 20% acidic and 80% alkaline. It is recommended that we consume approximately 20% acidic forming foods and 80% alkaline forming foods.

The acid in the acid/alkaline balance is not the same as stomach acid. A healthy stomach pH is acidic which is necessary for digesting food. What we are discussing here is the pH of the body's fluids, cells and tissues. Also, this is not about lemons and oranges being acidic as they are to begin with. Foods are either acid forming or alkaline forming within the body. Lemon happens to be the most alkaline forming food even though it starts out being acidic.

The diet of the average person needs to have more alkaline forming foods in it to be balanced. How is that achieved?

10 Tips for Creating an Alkaline/Acid Balanced Body

1. **Eat Lots of Vegetables and Fruit.** This is the one thing you can do that can make all the difference. Keep vegetables cut up in the fridge and have a big bowl of colourful fruit on your counter to snack on. Eat salad with your lunch and dinner; keep a salad made up in advance with all of the greens in it minus salad dressing, cucumbers and tomatoes which you can add later.

2. **Eat 80% alkaline foods, 20% acid foods by volume daily.** Look at the charts below and get to know which foods are acid and which ones are alkaline.

3. **Chew your food well**. Saliva is alkaline and you can produce 2 gallons a day!

4. **Drink 2 - 3 litres of pure water** (not from the tap) per day. Water alone can make all of the difference as many people are dehydrated and dehydration keeps in all of the toxins, which are acidic. Drinking lots of water will help flush these toxins out.

5. **Bodies function better with more oxygen.** This will help move the acids out of your body. Practice breathing deeply into your abdomen. Focus on your breathing without distractions. Lie down on your bed and breathe into your abdomen deeply and gently, practice doing this every day till you are doing it naturally all day every day.

6. **Avoid junk food;** it is filled with artificial sweeteners, preservatives, artificial chemical substances and food coloring, which are all highly acid forming as well. Additionally, your body must work very hard to eliminate these toxins.

7. **Find ways to create relaxation in your body and being.** Listen to the birds or relaxing music, meditate, walk in nature and do whatever it is that creates relaxation in you.

8. **Live in the light of the day.** We need sunlight and fresh air for they are essential for our health and wellbeing. Go for walks, open your curtains and go to bed early rise when the sun does.

9. **Get enough sleep** as insufficient sleep causes the body and mind to be overworked and unhappy, producing more toxins in the body and mind.

10. Just because a food is acid forming doesn't mean that it is unhealthy! **It is not about excluding an entire family of foods or any foods; it is all about creating balance.**

What are the Alkaline and Acid Foods?

Simply put: all you have to do is eat 80% vegetables and fruit, which are alkaline forming.

There are some exceptions which is why I have put together a chart to help you learn what they are. From my extensive research I found there was conflicting information on what are the acid forming and alkaline forming foods. Use the chart below as a general guide which may contain some discrepancies

The following is a colourful Acid/Alkaline chart list of common foods; not all foods as three pages are long enough. Do print and put on your fridge for easy reference.

ACID / ALKALINE FORMING FOODS

MOST ACID	LOWEST ACID	FOOD CATEGORY	LOWEST ALKALINE	MOST ALKALINE
Peanuts, Chick-peas	White Asparagus, Most Beans (Kidney, Navy, Red, Aduki, Lima, Garbanzo Mung, Fava, Pinto, White) String/Wax Beans, Zucchini, Split pea, Tempeh, Lentils, Chutney, Popcorn, Potatoes Peeled	Beans, Vegetables, Legumes, Pulses, Roots, Fruits	Brussel sprouts, Beets, Chives, Peas, Cilantro, Jicama, Kohlrabi, Cabbage, Okra, Mushroom, Carrots, Potato with skin, Squashes, Collards, Parsnip, Iceberg Lettuce, Pumpkin, Fresh Soy Beans, Eggplant, Artichokes, Sweet Corn, Cauliflower, Green Asparagus	Seaweed, Wheat Grass, Swiss Chard, Spinach, Dandelion Greens, Taro, Onion, Miso, Daikon, Celery, Burdock, Sweet potato, Yam, Lotus root, Garlic, Endive, Kale, Parsley, Arugula, Beets, Bell pepper, Broccoli,Turnip greens, Cucumber, Dark Green Lettuces, Peas
Cranberries, Sour Cherries, Jam, Jelly, Pomegranate	Blueberries, Cherimoya, Pickled fruit, Coconut, Plums, Prunes, Processed Fruit Juices, Green Bananas	Fruits	Bananas, Most Berries, Grapes, Currants, Dates, Gooseberry, Tomatoes, Grapefruit, Guava, Nectarine, Peaches, Persimmon, Avocado, Orange, Cherries, Rhubarb	Lemons, Lime, Umeboshi Plums, Cantaloupe, Melons, Figs, Raisins, Mango, Papaya, Kiwifruit, Pears, Grapes, Passion fruit, Apricots, Pineapple, Apples
White Rice, Barley, Rye, Pasta (white), Semolina, Wheat flour and bread, Pastries, Cakes	Kasha, Brown Rice, Spelt,Oats Buckwheat, Teff, Kamut, Farina, Tapioca, Triticale, Cornmeal, Barley	Grains, Cereals, Grasses	Quinoa, Wild Rice, Japonica Rice, Amaranth, Sprouted grains	Millet
Hazelnuts, Walnuts, Pistachios, Brazil nuts	Pine nuts, Pecans, Cashews, Peanut Butter, Tahini	Nuts, Seeds, Sprouts	Almonds, Seeds (most), Sprouts, Sesame Seeds, Chestnuts	Pumpkin Seeds
Table salt refined and iodized	Spices (most), Ginseng, Gelatin, Nutmeg	Spices, Herbs	All herbs, Vanilla, Cinnamon, Ginger Fresh	Cayenne, Baking Soda, Agar Agar, Pepper Sea Salt, Soy Sauce

Lard, Hydrogenated Palm, Chestnut, Cottonseed, Olive (processed), Fried Foods	Pumpkin seed, Grape seed, Sunflower, Canola, Almond, Sesame, Safflower	Oils	Only Cold Pressed Oils: Avocado, Coconut, Linseed, Primrose, Cod Liver, Olive, Flax Seed	
Beer, Alcohol, Soft Drinks, Coffee, Black Tea, Processed Fruit Juices Sweetened	Sake, Cocoa, Processed Fruit Juices Unsweetened	Beverages	Kombucha, Grain Coffee, Green Tea, Mu tea, Fresh Fruit Juices	Fresh Lemon Water, Mineral Water, Fresh Vegetable Juices, Herb Teas
White Acid Vinegar	Rice Vinegar, Balsamic Vinegar	Vinegars	Umeboshi Vinegar, Apple Cider Vinegar	Fresh Lemon Juice
All Artificial Sweeteners, Brown & White Sugar, Molasses, Maple Syrup	Carob, Honey Pasteurized, Unsulfured Molasses	Sweeteners	Raw Honey, Raw Sugar, Rice Syrup	Stevia
Mussels, Squid, Lobster	Fish, Shell Fish, Mollusks	Fish / Shell Fish		
Beef, Goat, Pork, Chicken, Deer, Veal, Rabbit, Pheasant, Bear, Lobster	Wild Duck, Goose, Turkey, Lamb, Organs, Venison, Boar, Elk, Turkey	Fowl, Meats, Wild		
Antibiotics, Psychotropics	Antihistamines, Most prescription medications	Therapeutic	Algae blue-green	Umeboshi Plums
Table Salt	MSG, Benzoate	Preservatives	Sulfite	
Processed Cheese, Cottage cheese, Ice Cream, Homogenized Milk	Cream, Butter, Cow Milk, Yogurt sweetened, Aged Cheese, Goats	Milk Cow/Breast	Ghee (clarified butter), Butter milk, Yogurt unsweetened	Breast Milk
	Rice Milk, Soy Cheese, Tempeh, Almond Milk Processed	Non-Diary	Almond Milk Freshly Made, Tofu, Soy Milk	
	Chicken Eggs	Eggs	Duck Eggs, Quail Eggs	

How to Test Your pH Balance

Testing your Saliva's pH

What you need:
- A roll of testing pH paper (pH strips with a range of 6.0-8.0 pH are best). Most Health Food stores and Pharmacies will have the pH strips.
- A plastic spoon (metal affects the pH).
- Fresh saliva.

Instructions:

1. For accurate results do not eat, drink or brush your teeth 30 minutes prior to the testing.
2. Before testing: swallow a couple of times to clear the mouth and stimulate new saliva; then put some saliva in the plastic spoon (do NOT to touch the pH paper to your tongue due to the chemicals in the paper).
3. Take a one inch strip of pH paper and dip it into the saliva.
4. Compare the color of your pH paper with the colour chart on the pH testing roll.

The lower the pH value below 7.0, the more acidic you are. To really learn about what is happening acid/alkaline wise in your body continue testing your pH for a few weeks. Do it first thing in the morning, afternoon, and at bedtime. This will show how the body is retaining the balance.

Testing half an hour after meals will show what that meal has done. Usually the saliva's pH will rise to 7.8 or higher. This is normal because there is an abundance of alkaline-rich minerals in saliva after meals.

Saliva that stays between 6.8 and 7.2+ pH all day, is within a healthy range.

Testing Your Urinary pH

Urine testing is more accurate. The ideal healthy pH range is between 6.5 - 7.0+. Urinary pH will usually be lower in the morning and higher in the evening. In the morning there may be more acid waste. You will likely see urine pH become more alkaline as the day progresses.

The pH of the urine is not as affected by digestive enzymes as salivary pH. However, the pH of urine can be affected by:

- An excess minerals and vitamins.
- Preservatives you ate.
- Pollutants breathed in.
- The food you ate.
- How much water you drank.
- Toxins being eliminated.
- Drugs taken.

Interesting Alkalizing Tid Bits:

- To neutralize a glass of cola with a pH of 2.5, you would need to drink 32 glasses of alkaline water with a pH of 10! Of course this isn't something you want to do. That is too much water.

- Beer has a pH of 2.5 so to neutralize it you would have to do the same as above. Hard spirits are also very acidic.

- Sprouted grains are more alkaline. Grains chewed well become more alkaline.

- Natural sugars from fruit are more alkaline. Sugar added to juice makes it acid forming.

- Agar Agar is a great alkaline substitute for acid forming gelatin.

- Lemon water is a very quick way to alkalize your body.

- Most mouthwashes are acidic and cause cavities. Baking soda is alkaline and is a good mouth wash. It neutralizes the pH level of the saliva making it more alkaline so the enamel of our teeth doesn't erode.

2 Recipes For Quick Alkalizing!

Balance the pH With Alkaline Foods

If you need to alkalize quickly; here are two recipes using two of the most alkaline forming foods: lemons and watermelon which are superfoods!
The most alkaline forming food you can eat is a lemon. Here is a simple way to get some quick alkalizing going into your body. Lemon juice has great digestive qualities so symptoms of indigestion such as heartburn, bloating and belching are often relieved. Also, lemons also help cleanse the body of toxins.

Lemon Water (AKA Sugar-free Lemon Aid)
Ingredients:
1 lemon
Water (clean water, not from the tap)
Stevia
Directions:
1. Wash the lemon well
2. Cut lemon in half, horizontally
3. Squeeze each half of a lemon
4. Add to 2 – 4 cups of water. The lemon juice can be diluted according to taste.
5. Add stevia to taste if desired.

Nutrition Tip: Fresh lemons are high Vitamin C, Dietary Fiber and low in calories. They have Vitamin B6, Calcium, Potassium, Copper, Thiamin, Riboflavin, Pantothenic Acid, Magnesium and Iron.

How many lemons to eat?

- Weighing less than 150 pounds, 1 lemon a day.
- Weighing over 150 pounds, 2 lemons a day.

> "The lemon is a wonderful stimulant to the liver and is a dissolvent of uric acid and other poisons, liquefies the bile, and is very good in cases of malaria. Sufferers of chronic rheumatism and gout will benefit by taking lemon juice. In pregnancy, it will help to build bone in the child."
> - Back to Eden, Mr. Kloss

Why No Sugar and Why Stevia?

Sugar Suppresses the Immune System – Sugar interferes with the body by overtaxing its defenses according to the Research at Natural Library of Medicine.

Stevia is a natural sugar alternative that nourishes the pancreas and has no calories. It is an herbal extract from the Stevia Rebaudiana leaf that has been shown to regulate blood sugar and blood pressure. www.realfoodforlife.com/stevia

Watermelon Juice

Here is a very easy and refreshing juice made from superfood watermelon.

Interesting Facts About Watermelons:

- Whole watermelons stored at room temperature had substantially more nutrients says a report in the Journal of Agricultural and Food Chemistry. Refrigerated watermelon, like 41 F (5 C) starts to decay after a week.
- Watermelon is the lycopene leader of fresh fruits and vegetables. *"There have been a few experimental studies on the role of lycopene in preventing or treating cancer. Some evidence suggests that cancers of the pancreas, colon and rectum, esophagus, oral cavity, breast, and cervix could be reduced with increased lycopene intake."* ~ Natural Medicine Journal
- Watermelon is a diuretic and was a homeopathic treatment for kidney patients before dialysis.
- Watermelons contain citrulline an ingredient that can trigger the production arginine, an amino acid that benefits the heart and blood circulation and immune systems. It helps relax the body's blood vessels, similar to what happens when a man takes Viagra, said scientists in Texas. More citrulline is found in watermelon rind (60%) and in yellow watermelons.

Watermelon Juice Recipe

Ingredients:
Watermelon, as much as you want; 1 cup diced watermelon is only 46 calories!

Directions:
1. Cut off the rind from the watermelon.
2. Simply cut up watermelon flesh into pieces.
3. Put into the blender (even if it has seeds in it).
4. Blend till totally juiced.
5. If there are seeds then strain while pouring.
6. Serve this in a tall clear glass as it is so beautiful.

My friend Karuna Sanghviin India has another way to make it if you do not have a blender. "Instead of using a blender, simply try mashing the pieces and strain it. You can add watermelon pieces to this and it tastes heavenly."

Millet Only Alkalizing Grain!

Millet is a gluten-free grain that provides a host of nutrients and has a sweet nutty flavour. **It is considered to be one of the most digestible and non-allergenic grains available.** It is one of the few grains that is *alkalizing to the body*.

It has always been a favorite grain of mine since I discovered it in my hippy days in the 70's!

Millet is the only alkalizing grain and it provides many nutrients (15% protein), has a sweet nutty flavor and is considered to be one of the most digestible and non-allergenic grains available and of course it is one of the powerfoods.

Millet History:
- First cultivated in Northern China in 4500 BC.
- Was the basic grain cultivated in China along with a few experiments in growing wheat and hemp.
- In ancient China millet was considered one of the five sacred crops.
- In approximately 2800 BC recorded writing, Fan Shen Chih Shu in explains how to grow and store the sacred grain.
- During the Han period, they drank millet wine, which was more popular at that time than China's native cup of tea.

Millet Today:

- Ranks as the sixth most important grain in the world.
- Sustains 1/3 of the world's population and is a significant part of the diet in northern China, Japan, Manchuria and various areas of the former Soviet Union, Africa, India, and Egypt.
- The Hunzas, who live in a remote area of the Himalayan foothills and are known for their excellent health and longevity, also enjoy millet as a staple in their diet.

Nutritional Information for 1 Cup Cooked Millet:

Calories 286
Carbohydrate (g) 57
Total fat (g) 2.4
Cholesterol (mg) 0
Saturated fat (g) 0.4
Sodium (mg) 5
Monounsaturated fat (g) 0.4
Thiamin (mg) 0.3
Polyunsaturated fat (g) 1.2
Niacin (mg) 3.2
Dietary fiber (g) 3.1
Magnesium (mg) 106
Protein (g) 8
Zinc (mg) 2.2
Data from wholehealthmd.com

Millet & Buckwheat with Sunflower Seeds

This is a favorite recipe of mine! It is very tasty and mostly alkaline (sunflower seeds and buckwheat aren't alkaline forming). Buckwheat with its full flavour enhances the light flavour of the millet.

Millet & Buckwheat with Steamed Vegetables

Ingredients:
1/4 cup sunflower seeds
1 cup millet
1/4 cup buckwheat
1/2 tsp. Himalayan salt or sea salt
2 1/2 cups water

Directions:
1. Sauté dry sunflowers seeds.
2. Add millet after a few minutes.
3. Sauté until golden brown.
4. Add buckwheat salt and water.
5. Bring to a boil and cover with a tight lid.
6. Simmer until all the water is absorbed – approximately 40 minutes.
7. Serve with your choice of vegetables.

Eat Greens to Create a More Alkaline Forming Diet

Greens on your plate will make your body great!

The highest value alkaline foods are greens.

They are an essential part of a healthy diet. There are so many greens such as leafy lettuce, spinach, Swiss chard, kale, collard greens, romaine lettuce, arugula, mustard greens and bok choy.

The extra benefits you get from the greens are that they are full of vitamins A, K, D, and E which are fat soluble.

To absorb these vitamins make sure to add a teaspoon of dietary fat, such as olive or coconut oil, nuts, or salad dressing. This will help your body assimilate all the nutrients in the greens. Vitamin K helps calcium and phosphorus bind onto the bone protein matrix.

All of the leafy greens are superfoods. https://www.realfoodforlife.com/superfoods

Start Your Day with a Green Smoothie!

Have you heard of the green smoothie revolution in food?

This is a great way to begin your day with a 100% alkaline meal. It all began with a search for better health for Victoria Boutenko's sick family and they are all very healthy now (www.rawfamily.com)

Green smoothies are actually very tasty even though they are green which sometimes scares people.

10 Reasons to Include Green Smoothies into Your Diet

1. More vegetables in your diet in a hidden way for those who think they don't like vegetables.
2. They are full of vitamins and minerals which you need for a healthy immune system
3. Alkaline forming for the body.
4. Filled with chlorophyll, this is nourishing.
5. Nutrients are more easily absorbed.
6. Have lots of fiber which we know we need.
7. Full of antioxidants which can help reduce chronic diseases, like heart and cancer disease.
8. Easy to digest when green smoothies are blended well so you will get all the nutrients.
9. Simple to make and quick too and they actually taste good.
10. Improve energy levels and reduce fatigue.

Watch me make a green smoothie on a video by going here: www.realfoodforlife.com/greensmoothie

To get all the benefits of a green smoothie it is best to eat, not drink, your smoothie. Digestion begins with the enzymes in the saliva in your mouth.

2 Green Smoothie Recipes

Here are a few recipes; the options for making a green smoothie are endless.

Orange Green Smoothie

This is a super easy smoothie to make and is good for a spring cleanse or any time.

Oranges are a very healthy superfood; they packed full of nutrients and health benefits. They are popular with athletes because they can be easily eaten for a burst of energy.

Golden flax meal: Two tablespoons provides 2430 mg of omega-3 fatty acids, as well as fiber, iron and potassium.

Ingredients:
2 oranges, peeled and chopped into pieces
3 cups spinach or 2 cups kale
1/3 – 1/2 cup clean water
1 Tbsp golden flax meal

Directions:
1. Put 1 1/2 oranges and greens in your blender.
2. Cover all ingredients with clean water.
3. Blend till smooth; use the liquefy button on the blender.
4. Put into a bowl or large glass.
5. Mix in flax meal and 1/2 chopped orange.
6. Eat your delicious green smoothie.

Alkalizing Apple Green Smoothie is Tasty for Breakfast and Healthy

This alkalizing apple green smoothie is so easy to make. It can be a very healthy breakfast or a tasty snack. It is simple to make with all alkalizing foods. Did you know that Apples, Spinach, and Pumpkin Seeds are all in the highest alkalizing category? So this is a very healthy way to start your day.

Apples: According to Chinese Medicine: Apples strengthen the heart, quench thirst, lubricate the lungs, decrease mucous and increase body fluids. **Spinach** is full vitamins like A, K, D, and E and a host of trace minerals. Choose organic spinach. Non-organic spinach is on the list of top foods with lots of chemical pesticides.

Ingredients:
1 apple, chopped
3 big handful of spinach
10 soaked almonds
1/4 cup soaked pumpkin seeds
1/4 - 1/2 cup pure water

Directions:
1. The night before soak the pumpkin seeds and almonds.
2. Put all in the blender and blend until smooth.
3. Add as little water as you need so you can eat with a spoon.

More Greens Are Good for Us Recipes

Here is a simple to make recipe of greens with a zingy lemon and a little crunch from the sesame seeds.

Steamed Greens Are Nutritious So Very Good for You and Tasty Too

Ingredients:
2 lbs. Swiss chard, or mustard greens or beet tops or spinach
2 tsp virgin olive oil
4 lemon wedges
1 Tbsp toasted sesame seeds

Directions:
1. Trim chard of any damaged leaves and tough stems.
2. Wash well to remove all sand.
3. Steam for 3 to 7 minutes until leaves are tender.
4. Remove from heat.
5. Put in a bowl and add oil.
6. Serve each portion with a lemon wedge and sprinkle with sesame seeds.

Note: I don't add salt to my greens as they are naturally high in sodium. 1 cup of cooked chard has 313 mg of sodium which is 13% of the daily requirement of sodium.

Vegetable Stir Fry for Dinner is Simple to Make and Delicious

A vegetable stir fry is a very simple and quick meal that tastes great. It can be healthy if you use good ingredients as this recipe does. Feel free to substitute the vegetables you like best.

All the vegetables including the garlic in this stir fry are alkaline forming.

Broccoli is high in fiber, protein, and detoxifying phyto chemicals. Broccoli is one of the many alkaline-forming foods that help prevent cellular damage to the eyes and may even slow the aging process.

Onions help relieve symptoms such as coughs, congestion asthma, and respiratory infections. A stir fry would not be the same without tasty onions.

Zucchini is sweet, easy, and quick to cook and they are antioxidant-rich and low in calories and a great addition to a vegetable stir fry.

Carrots are an orange crunchy super food with Vitamin A and other health benefits including beautiful skin, cancer prevention, and anti-aging.

Red bell peppers: Peppers have 2 times as much vitamin C as oranges. Red and yellow peppers have 4 times as much. They add colour and sweetness to this vegetable stir fry.

Vegetable Stir Fry Recipe

Ingredients:
- 1 onion
- 1 zucchini
- 1 carrot
- 1/2 red bell pepper
- 1 cup broccoli florets
- 1/2 Tbsp almond oil
- 1-4 cloves garlic
- 1-3 tsp Braggs or tamari

www.realfoodforlife.com

Handful fresh snap peas or 2 handfuls of spinach

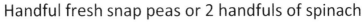

Directions:
1. Peel the onion and slice it.
2. Slice the zucchini into 1/2 inch rounds and then cut into half-moon shapes
3. Slice the carrot and red bell pepper.
4. Chop the garlic.
5. Heat on low heat the almond oil in a frying pan.
6. Add the garlic and onion to the pan, quick sauté for a few minutes.
7. Add the zucchini, and carrot, sauté a few minutes or until the carrot brightens in color.
8. Add broccoli; continue to sauté for 5 minutes, until the broccoli turns to a bright green colour.
9. Stir in Braggs, pea pods, and or spinach.
10. Cover the pan with a lid.
11. Turn off the heat and let the pan stand for a few minutes till the spinach is wilted.
12. Serve your vegetable stir fry with alkalizing millet.

A Salad A Day

A very simple way to get more greens into our diet is to eat one big salad each day and make sure it is filled with mostly greens. Here are two recipes.
Pumpkin seeds are so good that add a tasty crunch to this spring cleanse spinach salad.

Mixed Summer Greens Salad

Ingredients:
1 handful, Spinach
1 handful, Arugula
1/2 head, Red Leaf Lettuce
1/2 head, Green Leafy Lettuce
1 medium bunch of Parsley
3 Celery pieces, chopped
1 medium Cucumber, sliced in rounds
1/4 cup soaked or roasted Pumpkin Seeds

Directions:
1. Mix greens together in a bowl.
2. Top with celery, cucumber and pine nuts.
3. Serve with Mint salad dressing.

TIP: If you are planning on this lasting for the next day, do not mix the cucumber in or the salad dressing. Put then cucumber in a bowl on the side and add to each serving of salad. A mix of the basic ingredients without the cucumber will last 3 days in the fridge.

Lemon-Mint Salad Dressing

It is best to make your own salad dressing.
Here is a salad dressing with greens in it! The mint
adds a refreshing flavour.

Lemons' health benefits are
immense. To begin they are
acidic to the taste but are
alkaline-forming in the body. In
fact, they are one of the most
alkaline-forming super foods; this
makes them great for balancing a
highly acidic condition in the
body. Also, they are full of many
health benefits.

www.realfoodforlife.com

Mint is a very tasty addition to this olive oil salad
dressing. This super food is full of many health benefits
from helping with digestion to increasing memory.

Ingredients:
1 ¼ cups olive oil
¼ cup fresh lemon juice
2 tbsp. fresh mint (or 2 tsp. dried)
Salt to taste
Few drops of stevia

Directions:
1. Blend all ingredients.
2. Add salt to taste and stevia to taste and re-blend.

Spinach Salad Is Healthy and Tasty for You and Popeye

This salad is filled with very alkaline forming spinach and it is so delicious.

Mandarin oranges add sweet juiciness to this spring cleanse spinach salad. The bonus is that they are a delicious super food full of health benefits.

Ingredients:
1 pound fresh spinach
1 avocado, diced
1/4 cup chopped soaked or walnuts roasted till golden
2 mandarin orange sections
Light Herb Lemon Olive Oil dressing

Directions:
1. Wash and trim spinach; pat dry with paper towels.
2. Combine lemon olive oil dressing with avocado cubes.
3. Toss spinach and walnuts with avocado and dressing.
4. Add mandarin orange sections and toss spinach salad again and serve immediately.

Light Lemon Olive Oil Salad Dressing Is Delicious & Healthy

This is a base recipe that you can make up different each time with a variety of herbs. What makes this light is the addition of water.

Extra-virgin olive oil (cold-pressed) is the best fat to use as a salad dressing. Do not use for cooking. It has a low smoke point and heat makes it susceptible to oxidative damage. Olive oil has so many health benefits I include some every day when I eat my salad.

Make sure you are using real olive oil. Learn about the olive oil fraud before buying olive oil. www.realfoodforlife.com/which-olive-oil-to-buy-the-olive-oil-fraud

Ingredients:
1 cup olive oil
1/3 cup lemon juice
1/4 cup water
1/4 - 1 tsp. salt
1 – 3 tsp. basil
1/2 - 1 tsp. marjoram
1/4 tsp. rosemary
Few drops of liquid stevia

www.realfoodforlife.com

Directions:
1. Put all ingredients into a blender; blend till smooth.
2. Put in a jar with a lid and refrigerate until using.

Acid Forming
Or
Alkaline Forming Foods?

Now that you have learned so much about acid/alkaline balance, do you know which group below is acid forming and which is alkaline forming?

I am sure you know that it is the beautiful coloured heart full of fruits and vegetables on the right that are alkaline forming.

ONE LAST MESSAGE!

It is important to eat healthy so we aren't getting sick frequently. The acid/alkaline principle is a good way to begin. A good eating program is simple; we need to eat more vegetables and some fruit. That way you get the 80% alkaline forming foods in to your diet. It is best not to get more then that as it is important to have a body being 20% acid forming

Do note there is nothing wrong with all acid forming foods like brown rice, beans, nuts and seeds. They are good for us too. We just need to make sure that they are not more than 20% of our meals.

There is much more to learn about the foods you eat. Most of us have food sensitivities and these are the foods to avoid.

"My passion is to help everyone, young and old get real food into their bodies. Out with the Junk Food and in with the Real Food!

I believe the day will come when people will look back and say: Remember when people used to eat stuff that came out of packages that was filled with chemicals?

I really do believe that will one day be true. I love inspiring and teaching others about Real Food."

~ Diana Herrington

Acknowledgments

Through the years,many have shared ideas,mentoring and support that have impacted my life,each in a different way. It'simpossible for me to thank everyone and I apologize for anyone not listed. Please know that I appreciate you greatly.

Randy Fritz helped me get healthier with his advice. Also making the website and books happen.

Dr Chen helped me regain my health with his Chinese herbal foods.

Wayne Rogers with his deep intelligence sharing what he just learned.

April Dery shared so many healthy tips with links to good articles.

Maureen Doram expanded my information about health food supplements.

Zahra Ismail has helped me for years with editing website articles and keeping my bookkeeping in order.

Rob Cooper for all he has done to help my website stay in tune and sharing healthy information.

Sharon Melvin has been a good friend to consult with, and her many helpful health ideas.

Rob Flood has always been there whenever I needed some ideas or support.

Health Blog – Adrian Lewis has been very inspiring with his huge website. Also, appreciate his help at bringing more traffic to Real Food for Life.

Dr Master Sha helped keep me grounded to do more of what I want to do.

Robert Cheeke is a big inspiration for me. He is a Vegan body builder.

Best Seller on Fire has been inspiring and very helpful to get this book published.

ADDITIONAL RESOURCES

That will help you to eat healthier.
Alkaline Diet Bootcamp
Will Transform Your Health in a Weekend

www.realfoodforlife.com/retreats/ alkalize-your-body-bootcamp

As you have purchased this book, we will have your email and send you a link to the courseso you can start right away.

ABOUT Diana

Diana Herrington has been sharing and researching healthy living and food in a big way since she healed from being unwell for 17 years. Her Real Food for Life website is very popular with over 350 very healthy recipes, over 100 Superfood articles, general health information, and many free webinars and online courses. She is very busy on her website creating more posts regularly. Still, she creates healthy meals and goes for walks every day even in the winter.

www.RealFoodforLife.com

Diana is behind the scenes,with social media getting her word out. On Twitter now know as X as @DancinginLife she has almost 42,000 followers, Facebook with 6,000 followers, Pinterest and Instagram.

Coaching is another area where Diana helps people create a healthy lifestyle. Many of her friends get free tips on how to eat and live healthier when they ask and are very happy.

"We all have our own choices to make. Mine is to make healthy choices." ~ Diana Herrington

More Health Resources

To help you to achieve success, visit:
www.RealFoodforLife.com

Learn How to Do a Cleanse with These Free   Detox Webinars
www.realfoodforlife.com/free-detox-webinar

In-depth courses on how eat healthy and create a body that are abundantly healthy.

www.realfoodforlife.com/courses

As I said earlier, this is the one principle that made a big difference in my journey back to wellness.
You can read my story here:
www.realfoodforlife.com/my-fibromyalgia-story

To learn more with a hands-on way of eating join
The Acid Alkaline Boot Camp

All the meals in the courses at Real Food for Life are balanced Alkaline/Acid.
www.realfoodforlife.com/retreats/alkalize-your-body-bootcamp

May you have many delicious balanced meals on you journey to a healthy Alkaline/Acid way of eating.

References

Greenliving Writer Page 2
https://web.archive.org/web/20190815185513/https://www.care2. com/
greenliving/author/dianah

WebMD Editorial Contributors Page 5
https://www.webmd.com/lung/what-to-know-about-acid-base-balance

Journal of Environmental Health Page 8
https://www.ncbi.nlm.nih.gov/pmc/articles/PMC3195546/

American Journal of Clinical Nutrition Page 8
https://www.ncbi.nlm.nih.gov/pmc/articles/PMC5946302/

Dr. Theodore A. Baroody Page 9
https://www.goodreads.com/en/book/show/151487

Dr. William Lee Cowden Page 9 https://
drleecowden.com/dr-cowden-bio/

Loren Cordain, Ph.D., professor/researcher Page 9
http://whole9life.com/wpcontent/uploads/2010/10/cordainbastos
dairy.pdf
Dr Susan Brown - Osteoporosis Education Project, Page 10 https://
www.betterbones.com/about/

James L. Lewis III, MD Page 10
https://www.merckmanuals.com/home/hormonal-and-metabolic-
disorders/acid-base-balance/acidosis

Karen Collins, MS, RDN, CDN, FAND Page 11 https://
www.aicr.org/resources/blog/breaking-down-the-association-between-
alkaline-diet-and-cancer/

Sugar Research at Natural Library of Medicine Page 23
https://www.ncbi.nlm.nih.gov/pmc/articles/PMC9471313/
#:~:text=Previous%20study%20has%20found%20that,the%20immune
%20system%20(92).

Natural Medicine Journal Page 24
https://www.naturalmedicinejournal.com/journal/lycopenes-effects-
health-and-diseases

Alkalizing to the body Page 26
https://www.realfoodforlife.com/alkaline-diet/